21st Century
Basic Skills
Library

KEEP IT CLEAN
ACHOO!

1

by Cecilia Minden, PhD

Cherry Lake Publishing • Ann Arbor, Michigan

Published in the United States of America
by Cherry Lake Publishing
Ann Arbor, Michigan
www.cherrylakepublishing.com

Photo Credits: Cover and page 1, ©Bronwyn Photo/Shutterstock, Inc.;
page 4, ©Beth Van Trees/Shutterstock; page 6, ©iStockphoto.com/
ktaylorg; page 8, ©iStockphoto.com/sitox; page 10, ©matka_Wariatka/
Shutterstock, Inc.; page 12, ©iStockphoto.com/timsa; page 14,
©iStockphoto.com/Bronwyn8; page 16, ©iStockphoto.com/kickstand;
page 18, ©3445128471/Shutterstock, Inc.; page 20, ©iStockphoto.com/
Fertnig

Library of Congress Cataloging-in-Publication Data
Minden, Cecilia.
  Keep it clean: achoo!/by Cecilia Minden.
     p. cm.—(21st century basic skills library level 1)
  Includes bibliographical references and index.
  ISBN-13: 978-1-60279-856-4 (lib. bdg.)
  ISBN-10: 1-60279-856-7 (lib. bdg.)
  1. Sneezing—Juvenile literature. I. Title.
  QP123.5.M56 2010
  612.2—dc22   2009048573

Cherry Lake Publishing would like to acknowledge
the work of The Partnership for 21st Century Skills.
Please visit www.21stcenturyskills.org for more information.

Printed in the United States of America
Corporate Graphics Inc.
July 2010
CLFA07

TABLE OF CONTENTS

4

Here Comes the Sneeze

Your nose begins to **tickle**.

Here it comes!

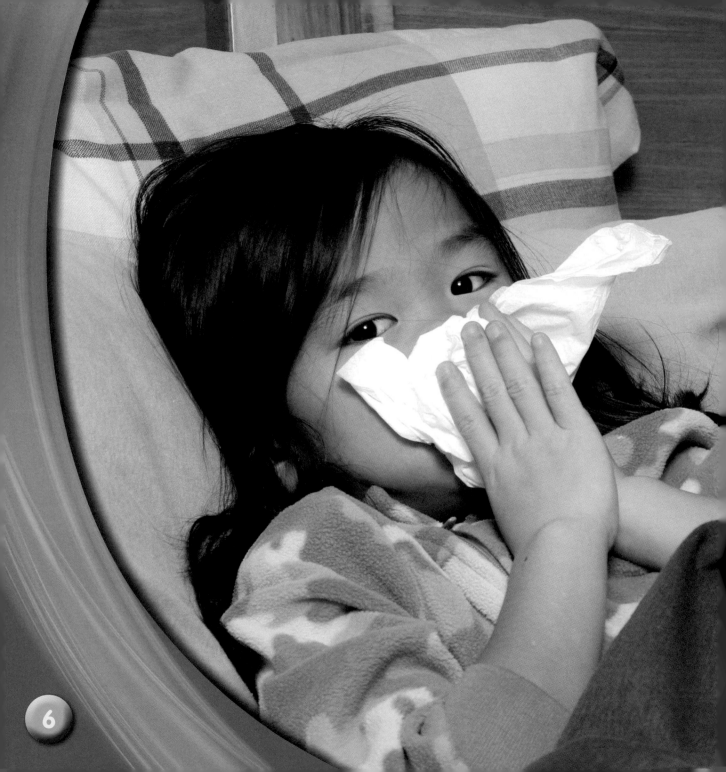

ACHOO!

Did you put something over your nose?

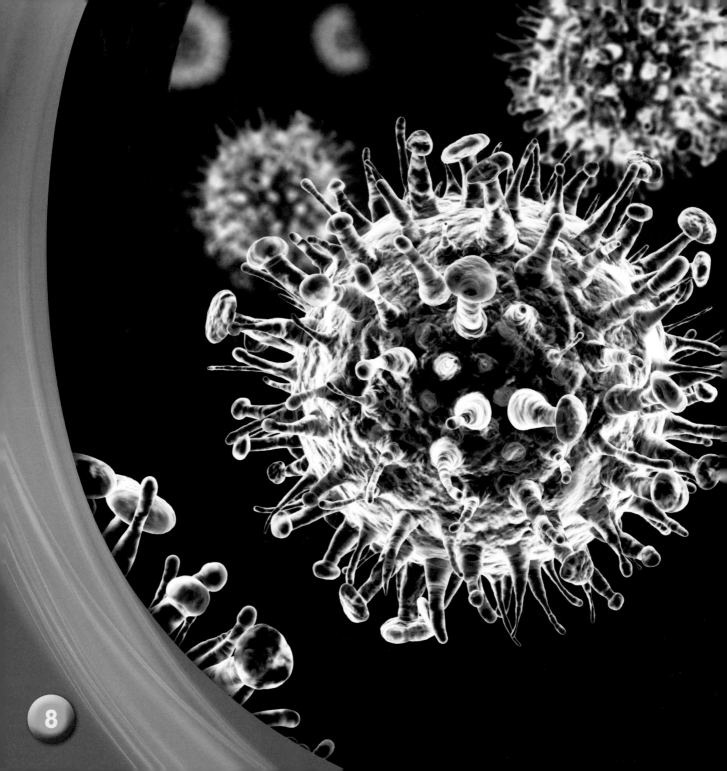

When we **sneeze**, we send out **germs**.

Germs can make us sick.

What Do I Do?

Do not use your hands.

Your hands will have the germs.

Use your arm.

This will help stop the germs.

You can also use a **tissue**.

Put the used tissue in the trash.

Keep It Clean

Your hands touch many things.

Keep your hands clean to stop germs.

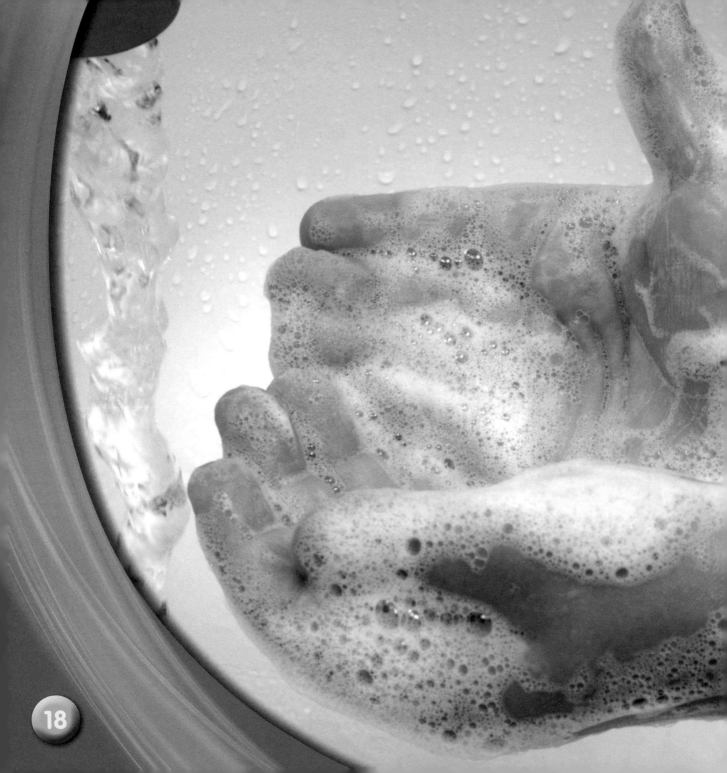

Wash with soap and water.

Be sure to wash for 20 seconds.

Remember!

Use your arm when you sneeze!

Find Out More

BOOK

Siy, Alexandra, and Dennis Kunkel. *Sneeze!* Watertown,
 MA: Charlesbridge, 2007.

WEB SITE

What Makes Me Sneeze?
kidshealth.org/kid/talk/qa/sneeze.html
Learn more about why people sneeze.

Glossary

germs (JERMZ) tiny living things we cannot see that
spread illnesses

sneeze (SNEEZ) explosion of air through the nose

tickle (TI-kel) a prickly sensation

tissue (TIH-shoo) soft paper cloth used to wipe your nose or
cover a cough or a sneeze

Home and School Connection

Use this list of words from the book to help your child become a better reader. Word games and writing activities can help beginning readers reinforce literacy skills.

a	have	seconds	trash
achoo	help	send	us
also	here	sick	use
and	I	sneeze	used
arm	in	soap	wash
be	it	something	water
begins	keep	stop	we
can	make	sure	what
clean	many	the	when
comes	nose	things	will
did	not	this	with
do	out	tickle	you
for	over	tissue	your
germs	put	to	
hands	remember	touch	

Index

About the Author

Cecilia Minden is the former Director of the Language and Literacy Program at the Harvard Graduate School of Education. She currently works as a literacy consultant for school and library publishers and is the author of more than 100 books for children.